"Clarity is Power" book series, is a collection of wisdom from thought-provoking Q and A with renowned Mahatria. His unique gift of answering questions spontaneously is captured in this book, offering life-changing insights.

The "Clarity is Power" series comprises 11 illuminating volumes, each addressing essential aspects of life:

1. Attitudes
2. Self-Discipline
3. Emotional Development
4. Relationships
5. Marriage
6. Parenting
7. Student Life
8. Career Growth
9. Leadership and Entrepreneurship
10. Spirituality
11. Faith

Mahatria Spiritualist | Thought leader | Diviner of infinitheism

For nearly three decades, Mahatria has empowered millions worldwide to achieve holistic abundance. His profound wisdom uplifts people in health, wealth, love, bliss, and spirituality.

infinitheism, the path divined by Mahatria, inspires breakthroughs for anyone who ardently desires abundance by transforming the human spirit to have faith in its infinite potential.

First published in India

Manjul Publishing House

• 2nd Floor, Usha Preet Complex,
42 Malviya Nagar, Bhopal 462 003 - India
• C-16, Sector 3, Noida, Uttar Pradesh 201301 – India
Website: www.manjulindia.com

Distribution Centres:
Ahmedabad, Bengaluru, Bhopal, Kolkata, Chennai,
Hyderabad, Mumbai, New Delhi, Pune

In association with:
infinitheism
3, 3rd Cross Road, R A Puram,
Chennai, Tamil Nadu, India
www.infinitheism.com

RELATIONSHIPS (CLARITY IS POWER)

by

This edition first published in 2016
Third impression 2024

ISBN 978-93-5543-428-9

Printed and bound in India by Thomson Press (India) Ltd.

RELATIONSHIPS

mahātria

CONTENTS

CONTENTS

1

Ouch! It hurts.
People you love the most hurt you the most.
What to do with hurt - express or suppress?

Hurt is a universal language. At the physical level it tells the dentist to ease up, and at the emotional level it tells a lover to change his approach. When hurt is expressed, it lets others know that they have gone too far. Telling someone that they have hurt you puts them on check. Letting others know that you are hurt and why are you feeling hurt helps others understand what is important to you.

Hurt is your private message. If it hurts you, it matters to you. Denying hurt is not being brave, but being merely reckless. The purpose of hurt is to limit the extent of the damage done to you. The role of hurt is to tell you that you have been damaged - physically or emotionally. It defines the limits of trespassing. Hurt teaches you to establish limits with others. Your hurt is a feedback to you and communicating it to others becomes a feedback to them. It shows you and others how much you can tolerate. These limits are especially important with people you really care about. People you truly love are the ones with whom you relate with your guards down and hence you are most vulnerable to be hurt by them. In fact, people you love the most have the power to hurt you the most. Conveying hurt helps people involved in a relationship to become more sensitive towards each other.

If you do not express yourself when others hurt you, then they have no way of knowing that you did not like what they did to you and with you. They would believe whatever they did was acceptable to you. So they keep repeating the same behaviour and continue the same approach. In due course hurt compounds and becomes complex. If you don't maintain boundaries, you will find others hurting you all the time, not because they are bad, but because they never knew that they were hurting you.

You avoid expressing your hurt because you do not want to admit that you can be hurt. You believe if the world knows that you can be hurt then it will take you to be vulnerable. So you keep denying your hurt, because you do not want to take any action that might leave you all alone, which is your worst fear. So you prefer to suffer with the person than without the person. Remember, expressing hurt as and when it happens will never take a person away from the relationship. But, if you keep continuously sweeping everything under the carpet for too long and then one day you will find dust accumulation of unmanageable proportion.

Expressing hurt when it happens is vital for keeping a relationship safe and honest. If you do not say 'No' to hurt WITHIN a relationship, then one day you will have to say 'No' TO the relationship. It becomes a major challenge to get people to stay away from your space, when you have been continuously pampering them by letting them to barge into your psychological space. It is difficult to assert yourself with someone who has accustomed themselves to violating your boundaries. Now, they will even claim that it is their right to do so.

The practice of prolonged usage defines ownership and rights. If you allow people to use a shortcut across your property, without posting a 'No Trespassing' sign, after few years that shortcut becomes a public way and you lose all claim to it.

If you want to know how some of your most valued relationships went off track, you need to look no further than the way you kept avoiding speaking out when you were hurt. You were betrayed by your own assumption that others will care enough for your feelings and will not hurt you. The truth is that people consider their feelings first. It is not that people are bad. It is just that people naturally tend to be selfish. They just want what they want. If you don't object, others will simply act in their best interest. If you allow others to exploit you, you will be exploited. If you allow others to take you for granted, you will be taken for granted. If you allow others to hurt you, you will be hurt. People treat you in life the way you teach them to treat you.

Your rights are not guaranteed, unless you are willing to defend them. If you don't learn to object, then you become inhibited about objecting. Most problems that you suffer would be solved if you could stand up for yourself at the time of your being hurt. Hurt can be a powerful relationship builder only if you do not deny it.

So, the next time someone hurts you, directly tell the person who caused it and do not make it a matter of gossip. Do not conceal it, deny it or pretend as if it did not matter. Do not punish others or plan a revenge to show you are tough. You were hurt - say so and leave it at that. What the other person will do when you tell him that you were hurt cannot be your concern. Expressing your hurt is your business. Do not let your fear of rejection silence you. Separate the hurt of the present from the hurt of the past. Do not get into the negative history between you and the other person - citing prior damages. Do not keep nagging. Remember that the person to whom you are expressing your feelings is someone you love and you want that person to have an opportunity to recover. Avoid overkill. Don't overdo and overact. Just say it and just let go.

Having expressed your hurt, forgive people who have hurt you. Forgiving is letting go of your hurt. Without forgiving you cannot grow. You cannot correct or alter what has already been done to you. Forgiving does not mean that you have to be in a friendship with people who have hurt you. It only means that you no longer allow your old hurt to be a cause for you to suffer. If you are holding on to your hurt to show others that they have injured you, you are only wasting your life. If you expect others to apologise for hurting you and wait until they do so, you will only prolong your suffering. You cannot delay your well-being by waiting for someone to become good. If you search your past looking for villains, be assured that you will find them, but you will not find peace. It is time to forgive and move on... Move on... You have nothing to prove. •

2

One of the girls working with me is 14 years younger than me. She recently lost her father and I see a daughter in her. She also calls me 'Daddy'. Shockingly, my wife is against this relationship. Kindly guide me.

Visualise the solar system. Visualise the Sun in the middle and all the planets orbiting around the Sun. With the same model let us view our life, our roles and our relationship with our roles. You represent the Sun and the roles you play represent the planets. The time you invest in a relationship, coupled with the emotional bondage you have for that relationship defines the status of the relationship. Higher the investment of time and emotions in a relationship, the closer they become to you... they represent the planets closer to the Sun in this relationship model. They become your Mars, Earth, Venus and Mercury. The lesser the investment of time and emotions in a relationship, the more they get distanced from you... they represent the planets away from the Sun in this relationship model. They become your Jupiter, Saturn and Uranus.

Relationships for which there are overflowing emotions and where there is a lot of interaction and also a lot of investment of time... there is a sense of ownership towards that relationship; these are called your Mercurian roles - the very strength and the very weakness of your life. Mercurian roles have a great influence on the emotional stability and instability of your life. Mercurian roles enjoy the lion's share of your time. It will be difficult to define your life without a reference to your Mercurian roles. They are not the other. They become your natural extension. They are almost you.

When a new relationship in your life, say starts as Jupiter, but with time, is inching towards Venus or Mercury, this very progression will emotionally unsettle your existing Venus and Mercurian roles. You will end up dealing with a lot of emotional issues. The arrival of a new Mercury is not even needed; just the possibility of a new Mercury is enough to unsettle those who are very close to you. As there are only 24 hours, the only way you can entertain a new Mercury or Venus is by taking away a part of the time and also attention from some of your existing Mercury and Venus. This makes your existing Mercurian and Venus roles very insecure... rightfully so. That's why when you develop a new friendship and also get obsessed with this new relationship, it emotionally tears apart your existing relationships.

Out of over excitement for a new found relationship, you straightaway give it Mercury status. You create an overnight Mercury in your life. Now, in order to find time for this new Mercury, you will have to reduce your time and attention to some of your existing Mercurian roles. This will cause tremendous heartaches to all your existing Mercurian roles. You will put your near and dear ones through sleepless nights, you would get emotionally drained and finally, helplessly you will drop the overnight Mercury, leaving it with lasting hurt.

Relationships that start as Uranus or Saturn and over a period of time gradually grow into Mars, Earth and Venus are the most stable of relationships. The longer a relationship takes to build into an intimate one, the more stable the relationship becomes. Relationships should never be like the overnight plants which grow at a sensational pace and die at the same sensational pace. Relationships should be like the trees that live for over a century. They take a lot of time in their formative years to grow, but are stable enough to weather the storms for a lifetime. At least with relationships, never try to do in 10 months what can be done in 10 years and never attempt to do in 10 days what can be done in 10 months.

When a relationship progressively grows into Mercury, though it may take time, it will happen without unsettling your existing Mercurian roles. Such relationships alone survive the test of time. So, I can be conclusive in saying, Mercury status should never be given. It has to be earned.

May you live your life in such a way that your heart and the heart of your loved ones always feel protected! May you live your life in such a way that the Sun - that's you - never feels claustrophobic! Nothing in the solar system suffers for space. May you live your life in such a way that there is as much harmony, order and precision in your relationships as there is in our solar system. ●

May you live your life in such a way that your heart and the heart of your loved ones always feel protected!

I have faced awkward situations with the opposite gender (male), when I went out alone. These incidents may be small, but these incidents have created a big fear in me. It disturbs me a lot. I want to come out of this fear. I want to become a very strong woman.

Fear is expanded F.alse E.vidence A.ccepted R.eal. Though it is only false evidence, because you have accepted it as real, it appears real. In your mind that rope has been accepted as a snake and hence to you it is snake. Just because you met a few people who were not good to you, you cannot assume that the whole world is bad. All men are bad is false evidence accepted real - that's your fear. In the same world where there are bad men, in that very world there are men who will come forward to protect you. Don't generalise life just because you encountered a few chance incidents.

If you have to kill a lion, you have to face it. Even if you have to lose some blood in the process that's the only chance you have got to kill the lion. Here the lion represents all fears. Don't die in instalments. That's what fear does to you - it kills you little by little. Avoid fear, it grows. Face fear, it goes. Go ahead in spite of fear. Repeatedly face what you fear and fear will be vanquished. Courage is just an initiative away from fear. Take that step forward in spite of your fear. Conquer fear fearlessly.

That which you do not face controls you, and that which controls you causes fear in you. You think you avoid the opposite sex because you fear them; in reality, because you are not facing the opposite sex, you develop fear of men. You do not avoid your Dad because you fear him; because you avoid him, you begin to fear him. Just because you are going to die one day, you don't stop living. Do you? Just because you fear something, don't stop facing it.

More than 95% of everything you've feared has never happened. So become aware of what fear is and overcome the fear of fear. The purpose of fear is to warn you of a situation that is unfamiliar to you. It pre-empts danger and initiates the physiological responses needed to face or escape the situation. Fear is actually a protector. Fear is a message, not a weakness. Understand your fear. Use your fear as a guide to help you understand and prepare for a challenge and not as an excuse for abandoning it. It is important to be brave in the face of fear and act in spite of it. Confidence is your belief that you will make it through in spite of your fear. You destroy confidence by giving in to fear, and you destroy fear by giving in to confidence. It is okay to be afraid, but it is not okay to escape. Face it. Courage is not the absence of fear, but the ability to go ahead in spite of fear.

Die by the will of God, and not by the fear of men. This world is far better than what a few scoundrels try to make us believe. Plunge into the world and face it. ●

Courage is
just an initiative away from fear.
Take that step forward
in spite of your fear.
Conquer fear fearlessly.

4

Which is more important in life - love or happiness?

Where there is love, happiness is not guaranteed; but where there is happiness, love is felt.

Love without happiness is a mere sentiment. You get hurt for everything, it instigates your ego, there are arguments, you are all the time doing expectation management, there is transaction in that love.

Love that is devoid of happiness is very possessive. Anybody who is in love, but is not happy in life, cannot leave you happy in life.

In the possessiveness drama that love plays out, love turns out to be a pain.

And for a person who knows to be happy in life, love is felt. There will be humor and ego doesn't get provoked that easily!

If you are happy in life, even in a worst situation, you will be able to move on... You will re-anchor yourself to happiness quickly.

Once happiness becomes, the rootedness, the anchor, love will become a byproduct. Love will be felt; you don't have to separately embrace it. Love emanates as a fragrance on its own from a happy person.

So, look at any relationship through the spectacles of happiness, love will blossom on its own accord.

We say, 'Happy New Year!', 'Happy Birthday!', 'Happy Anniversary' etc.... For everything we add 'happiness'. So, should we not anchor ourselves on happiness?

The lingering question should be - "How can I be a happy parent?" "How can be a happy boss?" "How can I be a happy spouse?" ...

When you become a happy spouse, you create a happy marriage and can love be far away?! When being with you for your children is the happiest experience, guiding them will not be difficult.

A lot of you look forward to being with your friends, because that's probably the happiest relationship for you. If home can become the happiest place...

What if you have a way by which you can make learning a happy experience... If you are a happy teacher and you have happy ways to teach, then learning becomes a happy experience.

I cannot understand how you can go to the most sacred place of worship and forget to smile there! Even spirituality should be 'Happy spirituality'.

When life is lived through the spectacles of happiness, love is taken care. You don't have to do anything exclusive for that. The other way round, is not true. So, anchor your life to happiness, love will follow.

If we can bring about this one shift in our lives, to see life through the spectacles of happiness, this world will be a better place to live in. ●

5

> *My father, over the past few years, has become non-functional - both at home and at work. It seems he has lost interest in life. At times this seems annoying, intentional and brings tears because he was a sharp contrast to everything written above. How do I bring back a smile on his face?*

Why do people lose interest in life? Either they think nobody needs them anymore, or they have nothing to look forward to in life.

Your love for your father is evident in the very question. Now your challenge is to ensure that you stay anchored to love and not keep shuttling between love and hate. Happily work with your father without giving up. It is time to mother your father. What's not possible for love! And, if love cannot, nothing else can.

Now, you will have to introduce touch in the relationship. He has to understand you all still respect him and you need him. The language of love is touch. No matter through how many other senses you express love, love understands only touch. Create enough contexts to touch him. Sit next to him, occasionally take his hands into yours, rub shoulders with him, give him an odd massage - not just you, get the whole family involved in touching him. Initially there will be a lot of resistance from him, but you will begin to see a change.

Talking is sharing. Listening is caring. Listen to understand and communicate to be understood. Bring a lot of conversational communication into the relationship. Again, initially he will not open up. He will only reply in monosyllables and sometimes be indifferent too. Communication has moved empires. Your father will also move. Initially he will reject all your initiatives, but you persist. Persistence will break any resistance. He will open up. Be patient.

The mantra is LONG ENOUGH. Communicate long enough. Express your love long enough. And write to me after a few weeks and give me the joy of knowing that he has finally smiled. Have faith in your love. ●

The language of love is touch. No matter through how many other senses you express love, love understands only touch.

6

I am a single woman in
my late 20s. Of late,
I find myself seeking attention
especially with men.
How do I deal with this?

A human being is not just flesh and bones. They are not just a series of chemical reactions. They are not just a bundle of hormones, biological parts and certain enzymes. Beyond everything, a human being is a bundle of energy. Energy manifests itself as heat energy, light energy, electrical energy, etc. Though energy is neither created nor destroyed, it can always be transformed from one form to another form of energy. This is simple physics.

Similarly, energy manifests through every human being as male and female energy. Both, man as well as woman is a combination of male and female energy. A select few, by their spiritual and yogic endeavours, have transformed themselves to a state referred to as *Ardhanareeswara*; in them their male and female energy is in a state of perfect balance. They are enough unto themselves. They are complete unto themselves. In all the ways, they are not dependent on anything outside of them. They are in a perfect state of unity. But, this is a minuscule minority. These people are the special gifts of existence to mankind.

Have you noticed, even when thousand incomplete people come together, the entire thousand still feel incomplete. On the contrary, in the presence of that ONE complete soul, the entire thousand feel complete. Isn't one SUN enough to be a source of energy for all forms of life?

Then how come there are so many sex scandals in the name of spirituality? Many self-proclaimed men sit on spiritual altars, still struggling with their energy imbalances. Arriving isn't arrived. Striving but not yet there. So their guise of being a Yogi can cheat the naked eye of the world and their followers, but the impulses of their energy imbalance takes them over and makes them stoop to bodily needs, and there lies their fall.

However, the overwhelming majority will have the male-female energy imbalance. This very imbalance creates the impulses in man and woman to seek the company of the opposite sex, so that in each other's presence the mutual imbalances may be balanced. So, by design, seeking the attention of the other sex or feeling attracted towards the opposite sex is as natural as feeling thirsty or hungry. It is a natural impulse. In fact, it is the male energy imbalance in a male body that drives men into homosexuality, and similarly female energy imbalance in a female body makes them seek another female. In all other cases, in search of that energy balance, you will be drawn towards the opposite sex.

But here comes the greatest blessing of being born as a human being. Animals, beyond bodily contact, don't have many ways to relate with the other. But man can see in another woman a great friend; a foster mother; a sister he always craved for; a daughter he is willing to groom; a colleague with whom he enjoys teamwork; an intellectual to discuss life; a potential you are willing to mentor. A woman can still find herself in the company of the opposite sex through so many dignified ways. This, to me, is one of the greatest blessings of being born as a human being.

If we only seek from each other the contact of the flesh, it seems so animalistic. The more intimate a man and a woman get, the closer they become, it will only culminate in a bodily relationship, sounds so animalistic. It seems to belittle the very dignity of human relationships. It shakes the very foundation of human relationships. Of course, that's what we have done from time immemorial. Why vulgarise the dignity of relationships with the opposite sex, when we could each be a bird with one wing embracing the other, so that we could fly together. I can show you some amazing relationships, called by various labels (friends - being the most popular of all), between the opposite sexes, who bring great dignity to man-woman relationships.

For us to experience the energy balance, we have to only let each other into each other's space. It doesn't have to become the need of the flesh. A relationship, even be it marriage, where the other relates with you only for the sake of the flesh, is nothing more than an animalistic relationship. Be with everyone. Relate with everyone. Relationships with the opposite sex actually act as exceptional mirrors unto you. You learn so much in reflecting each other. There is completeness in each other's presence. So, gift yourself those moments. But the moment the need of the body takes over, become aware, you or the other is stooping into becoming an animal. There is a line defining everything in life, and as long as we don't cross the border, everything is right. Once we cross the border, everything is wrong.

Develop a very strong value system and willpower. They would protect you at all times. Let 'you' belong to everybody, but let your 'body' belong to only one. Love all, but belong to only one. ●

“

Why vulgarise
the dignity of relationships
with the opposite sex,
when we could each be a bird
with one wing embracing the other,
so that we could fly together.

7

Why do people cheat their own family members or friends for the sake of money? Don't they realise they are doing wrong?

Cheating is wrong. It doesn't matter for the sake of what. It does not matter whether one cheats his own family members or his friends.

Duryodana once said, "I know what is right, but I am not able to indulge in it. I know what is wrong and I am not able to avoid it." A degree of Duryodana exists in most people. Wrong and wrong doers will continue. There was never a time without them and there will never be a time without them. They will continue to walk the planet. Even when Krishna was around, there was a Duryodana; in Gandhi's times there lived a Godse, and a community crucified Jesus, who epitomised nothing but love. From the time when man lived in the caves to now, a prophet wakes up every morning, only to see there is a little more evil in the world. Life is all about opposites. Without a background we won't appreciate the foreground. Bad, is the very context by which we understand what is good.

However, 'somebody cheated us' is only half the story. 'Something about us was cheatable' is the other half of the story. 'Somebody misappropriated funds' is only half the story. 'Some loopholes were there in the system that allowed misappropriation' is the other half of the story.

While one half of the story involves the other, who is only in the circle of our concern, the other half of the story involves us, and we are very much in the circle of our influence. So, let us first correct our side of the story. Let us first overcome our own vulnerabilities rather than continuing to be susceptible to the exploitation of others.

Rather than asking, why there are burglars in the world, let us make our home burglar-proof. 'Let there be no more Duryodanas in the world' is too hypothetical. Instead, let us be Arjunas to protect ourselves, as well as, protect righteousness. Prophet Muhammad put it this way, "Tie your camel first, then put your trust in Allah." ●

“

'Somebody cheated us'
is only half the story.
'Something about us was cheatable'
is the other half of the story.
Let us first overcome
our own vulnerabilities rather than
continuing to be susceptible
to the exploitation of others.

mahātria

8

Of late, I have been having problems with my friends. They never seem to understand me. They don't do for me, what they expect out of me. I get this feeling that I have been taken for granted. Kindly give me a solution.

An important realisation in relationship is to understand, 'People treat you in life the way you teach them to treat you in life'. So often, in the initial stages of a relationship, we take the nastiness of people with a lot of passivity. We don't tell them even if their behaviour is hurting us. They assume this behaviour of theirs is acceptable to us. We allow them to treat us as a doormat for too long and when it reaches an unbearable threshold, we begin to scream - foul, foul! You don't have to get even with people. But help them to know when they cross the line. It will do good to you, to them and to the relationship as a whole. Tell people who cause the hurt, that it hurts.

Rely on open communication. Don't make gossip out of your relationship issues. If a friend matters to you, don't keep discussing him/her with others. That's not being fair to the friend. Deal with the person involved directly. You cannot solve an issue without involving the person who is causing the issue. Rely on open-minded, direct communication. Either you will clarify or you will get clarity.

Above all, the root trouble in relationships is that nobody will know what your expectations are, unless you tell them. Instead of telling them what your expectations are, you tend to assume that they know it, which leads to so many disappointments in relationships.

For example, if your friend is with you all the time, you feel he is always interfering. If he leaves you alone, you feel he cares for you no more. So, what do you want him to do? Clarify your expectations.

If potato fry is cooked, then you scream, why everyday potato? So, potato is stopped in the house. Now you scream, you make potato no more. How are people at home suppose to know that you want potato once a week - not more and not less? Clarify your expectations.

For your birthday, if your friend didn't call at midnight, you get offended. If she does, you feel your sleep was disturbed. So, why don't you say it clearly - what you want? The fact is, so often even we don't understand what we want, but we expect others to understand what we want even without saying it. Funny! Very, very funny! So, clarify your expectations. ●

You cannot solve an issue without involving the person who is causing the issue.

9

My father,
mother and wife -
all three are very
possessive of me.
I am not able to balance
between the three.
Please help me out.

When three children have only one toy to play with, the toy will obviously be torn apart and there will be no harmony amongst the children. The situation in your family is no different.

First and foremost of all, we all actually enjoy, though secretly, others being possessive of us. It makes us feel important. We feel suffocated only when it becomes too much to handle. So first examine if you really want to solve it.

Secondly, understand that you can never be at peace with yourself if you try to please everyone around. Also, it is not possible to please those who are not at peace with themselves. Instead of trying to please everybody and losing your peace in the process, take clear standpoints - what can be can be, and what cannot be cannot be. There is a time for parents, a time for your wife, a time for the family as a whole, a time for yourself, etc... There is a time and season for everything under the sun. The most essential aspect of balancing one's time between seemingly equal priorities lies in one's ability to take standpoints. What is possible is possible and what is not is not.

Most importantly, your parents and your wife have a very narrow definition of the world. Expand the size of their world. Expand the definition of their world. Get your parents involved in satsangs - a spiritual fraternity; urge them to take evening walks in nearby parks, get them to visit relatives, get a puppy or an aquarium, get some potted plants... expand their world. Encourage your wife to pursue her talents, learn new proficiencies; send her to some coaching class; even if she is reluctant to work full time, encourage her to work part-time... expand her world. When their world expands, they will find new friends and hence more toys to play with. What happens to old toys when children get new toys? Beware!

Instead of trying to please everybody and losing your peace in the process, take clear standpoints - what can be can be, and what cannot be cannot be.

10

I generally observe in myself and in a lot of people that expectation from oneself is abysmally low and expectation from others is extraordinarily high. How to correct and get this balance right?

Expectations are born from the conditioning of your past and the resultant reactions that are projected into the future.

For example: You always admired your mother for her discipline. And, now you are married. Now, you expect your wife too to be disciplined, because you benchmark her with your mother. But your newly wedded wife, on discipline, never makes the grade. So, you are dissatisfied with her and she is frustrated with you.

"My father has always been honest and transparent. The problem with you is that you never tell me the whole stuff about your life," the wife complains to her husband. "Look at your brother's handwriting - it is a piece of art, and look at yours," the mother nags the daughter. "In my earlier organisation we never used to operate like this," cribs the new General Manager. "In America we don't have these issues," cries the NRI about India.

Expectation isn't a problem;
benchmarking expectation is.

You give your mother a '10 on 10' on discipline and hence you are not satisfied with your wife, who is tottering at 4 or 5. Hey, please understand that for her 5 is her 100% score - for her nature, temperament, upbringing, and conditioning, she will never make beyond 5 on discipline. This is her, and this will be her. There must be some other quality on which your wife must be a perfect 10 and your mother won't make the necessary grade. The husband may never be as transparent as your father, but he may be very selfless in financially aiding the family. The daughter may outperform the son in singing. You believed in better growth prospects here than the previous organisation, and that's why you are here. After all, India doesn't have some of the issues that the world has.

No one is inferior to others on all counts, and no one is superior to the rest on all measures. We all have our pluses, and we all have our minuses. No one is zero-defect. No one is all-defect. Stop focussing on isolated qualities. Start relating to the whole being.

However, there is a twist in the tale. When I am dissatisfied with others it makes me unhappy, but when I am dissatisfied with myself it helps me grow. When I benchmark others with my expectations, it leaves me dissatisfied with others and thus affects my happiness.

When I benchmark myself with my expectations, the dissatisfaction created propels my growth and development.

So, on all matters rate the world on '5' and rate yourself on '10'. Not that the world is any less capable or you are super-human, but because... Without happiness there is no life. So, expect less from the world. Without dissatisfaction there is no growth. So, demand more from yourself.

Proclaim to your beloved, "I am satisfied with your love. I, from my part, will find more ways to love you." ●

11

You say that expecting from others leads to disappointment. There are some relationships where the natural tendency is to expect. How can we refrain from expecting from our spouse or children?

Human predicament is in mismanaged expectations whether it is employer-employee relationships, in customer-vendor relationships, in parent-child relationships, in man-woman relationships. I don't want to sound too impractical by asking you to drop your expectations, but I want to take the pragmatic approach in telling you to manage your expectations better.

Realise that a mango tree is a mango tree. It was meant to be a mango tree; it will remain a mango tree, and from it you can only get mangoes - irrespective of your expectations, it can only produce mangoes. People are what they are. An organisation is what it is. Life is what life is. You expect people to be other than what they are and get frustrated with them. You expect an organisation to be other than what it is and get frustrated with it. You are expecting oranges from a mango tree and getting frustrated about not getting oranges. But is it the fault of the mango tree? This is what I call mismanaged expectations. If you think no organisation is giving you the right work environment, then why don't you start an organisation of your own and run it on your terms - create the environment you want. Find a tree according to your expectations or groom your own tree.

If you want peaceful progress in life, follow these guidelines:

One, define your expectations. More often than not, we ourselves aren't sure as to what we are expecting. We order an item from the menu card and seeing what the person at the adjacent table is eating we think 'maybe I should have ordered that'. So, first stop being confused yourself, lest you confuse the world around you.

Two, clarify your expectations explicitly. So often, others don't even know what you are expecting from them, then how can they fulfil it for you? Life is already complex. Let us not complicate it further. Please simplify life for others by clarifying your expectations clearly and explicitly.

Three, in case your expectations are not fulfilled, check if you are expecting oranges from a mango tree. If you find you are only expecting mangoes from a mango tree, then keep communicating long enough; keep clarifying your expectations patiently. Sure enough, patience and perseverance will eventually bear fruit. If this isn't the case, for instance, in key relationships where you cannot change the tree, learn to accept the mango tree as a mango tree and change your expectations according to the tree. It will give you peace. For your own sake, develop a taste for mangoes. In cases like organisations, where change is possible, find a tree according to your expectations. Rather than trying to change the world, change what is within your control - that is your own self. This will give you peaceful progress.

Importantly, the greatest learning in expectation management is, turn all the expectations you have of the world onto yourself. When expectations are directed towards the world, your peace and progress is at the mercy of the world. Turn them onto yourself, and you will be in control of your life.

Above all, always remember, neither will all your expectations be fulfilled, nor will all your expectations remain unfulfilled. Often, He will upset your plans in order to execute His plans for you. You go after oranges and I'll go after mangoes, remembering, it is not my will, but it is Thy will that will be done. ●

12

I do everything
for my brother and
the only thing he does in
return is to fight with me.
Help me.

First understand that every relationship is a training ground for other relationships. Please also understand that people treat you in life the way you teach them to treat you.

As you grow in life, you will meet a lot more people with the attitude of your brother. See your brother as an opportunity to learn to deal with people of his kind.

In fact, every time parents complain of sibling rivalries, I suggest to them, “Keep away. Let them learn to sort it out themselves. Nothing like the domestic grooming grounds.” You can protect the younger from the elder at home, but what will you do at school? The younger will be thrown into a world of bullies and she has to learn to confront and deal with all of them. You cannot be there all the time. In fact, you must not be there all the time. You are depriving the child of her grooming grounds. The elder too has to learn that he cannot get his way all the time. His leadership too will be seasoned through the little one. When you represent the child to the teacher, an opportunity has been lost for the child to learn to communicate with people she looks up to. She will, in the future, encounter such life situations and here are the training opportunities.

People say my boss is too harsh. Unless you are married to him, you don't have to live a lifetime with your boss.

While working with him, learn to deal with him, learn to manage your manager, don't let your boss, boss around with your emotions, learn to express yourself when there is disrespect. He is not the last one of his kind in the world. You will encounter many more such people in the world and here is a learning opportunity.

The other says, "The work ethics of the new generation is not acceptable." But you will have to lead the new generation. They are the future. Find out what makes this generation different from the earlier. How have their needs changed? What motivates them? What do they seek? You may not always get the team you seek and yet you are made responsible for the team's success. Here is an opportunity to polish your leadership. Make the most of such a team. Let them grow out of you and you too can grow out of them. The old saying is: "Good decisions come from life's experiences, and life's experiences come from bad decisions." Let the new saying be: "Good teams are born from good leadership, and good leadership is born out of bad teams."

Hey sister, your brother is grooming you into a more seasoned human being. One day in life, you will look back and thank him for all the maturity you gained out of relating with one such character - your brother. ●

People treat you in life the way you teach them to treat you.

13

I thought I had forgiven my best friend who had wronged me, only to realise later that the feelings of hurt keep resurfacing. Please tell me how do I truly forgive her and release this hurt.

First and foremost, remember forgiveness is not something you are doing for the benefit of your friend, but for your own benefit. You cannot forget. Deep memories are never lost. But you can forgive. Change the feelings associated with the incident and the person in that incident. By doing so you may continue to have a memory-recall of that incident, but you will never have an emotional-reliving of the incident. The scars will remain, but the injury would be gone.

As long as I don't change the feelings associated to the incident and the person involved in that incident that caused me hurt, I will continue to relive the same emotions. If she is your best friend, as you had stated, then realise that the person is much bigger than the instances of what happened between the two of you. Recall and relive the hundred special moments between the two of you, instead of the ten disturbing moments. Don't let the thorns blind you to the roses. ●

14

I am in love with a girl
but I keep doubting her
all the time, which
I know isn't right.
How to correct myself?

Persistent doubting is the most certain way to ruin your life, her life and also the relationship. Once you develop this attitude of doubting, it's not only going to affect your relationship with her and other people, eventually it will also start affecting your relationship with God.

Trust and peace are intertwined. I don't know if you will gain anything at all through persistent doubting, but for sure you will lose your peace and also disturb the peace of all around. I always reiterate, "Your judgement of me reveals a lot more about you than me, for, your judgement is born out of your background and not mine." Lack of trust and persistent doubting is because you feel less secure about yourself. It has nothing to do with the other. Your inferiority complex must be addressed. You are either feeling she is too good for you or feeling that there will be better men who will be interested in her. No matter where she changes and how much she changes, you will still suffer. You must change. You must learn to trust. You much believe her. You should start focusing on her intentions rather than her actions.

You need to remind yourself, "Much after her life and my life has become our life, there is still her life and my life."

Only when she invests enough time in 'her' space and you invest enough time in 'your' space, both of you will have the best of times in 'our' space. You cannot cage a person and expect to enjoy a deep relationship. Deep relationships come with freedom. Freedom comes with trust. Trust ensures peace. And love grows best from a peaceful heart. More than for her sake, more than for the relationship's sake, for your own sake learn to trust and give up this attitude of persistent doubting.

While mother is a matter of fact, father is a matter of faith. Nothing moves forward in life without the attributes of trust, belief, faith... always focus on the intentions of a person and never be cheap enough to assign your own meaning to the actions of people. By liberating yourself from the clutches of persistent doubting, you will liberate her from the clutches of your possessiveness.

Though the stem, branches, leaves, flowers, and fruits can be experienced and enjoyed by everybody, the roots belong only to the earth. Though your girl will be experienced and enjoyed by everybody in every role, you will always be her man.

Doubt enough till you trust.
Having trusted, stop doubting.